AF270473

Pecos Bill

BY MARLEY RICHMOND

Kids Core

An Imprint of Abdo Publishing
abdobooks.com

abdobooks.com

Published by Abdo Publishing, a division of ABDO, PO Box 398166, Minneapolis, Minnesota 55439. Copyright © 2024 by Abdo Consulting Group, Inc. International copyrights reserved in all countries. No part of this book may be reproduced in any form without written permission from the publisher. Kids Core™ is a trademark and logo of Abdo Publishing.

Printed in the United States of America, North Mankato, Minnesota.
102023
012024

Cover Photo: Silver Screen Collection/Moviepix/Getty Images
Interior Photos: Weerachai Pattala/Shutterstock Images, 4–5, 28 (bottom); Tom Reichner/Shutterstock Images, 7, 29 (top); Bob Pool/Shutterstock Images, 8; Tongpool Piasupun/Shutterstock Images, 10–11; Joseph Sohm/Shutterstock Images, 13; Melvin Sandelin/Shutterstock Images, 14; Roschetzky Photography/Shutterstock Images, 17 (top left); Amanda Mohler/Shutterstock Images, 17 (top right); Kris Wiktor/Shutterstock Images, 17 (bottom left); Lindsay Jubeck/Shutterstock Images, 17 (bottom right); Nicola Fusco/Alamy, 18, 28 (top); RKO Radio Pictures/Photofest, 20–21, 29 (bottom); Cary Meltzer/Shutterstock Images, 23; Impress/United Archives GmbH/Alamy, 24; Blank Archives/Hulton Archive/Getty Images, 26

Editor: Angela Lim
Series Designer: Katharine Hale

Library of Congress Control Number: 2023939752

Publisher's Cataloging-in-Publication Data

Names: Richmond, Marley, author.
Title: Pecos Bill / by Marley Richmond
Description: Minneapolis, Minnesota: Abdo Publishing, 2024 | Series: Tales from Americana | Includes online resources and index.
Identifiers: ISBN 9781098292874 (lib. bdg.) | ISBN 9798384910817 (ebook)
Subjects: LCSH: Pecos Bill (Fictitious character)--Juvenile literature. | Frontier and pioneer life--Juvenile literature. | Adventure and adventurers--Juvenile literature. | Tall tales--Juvenile literature. | Folklore--Juvenile literature. | Ranching--Juvenile literature.
Classification: DDC 398.22--dc23

CONTENTS

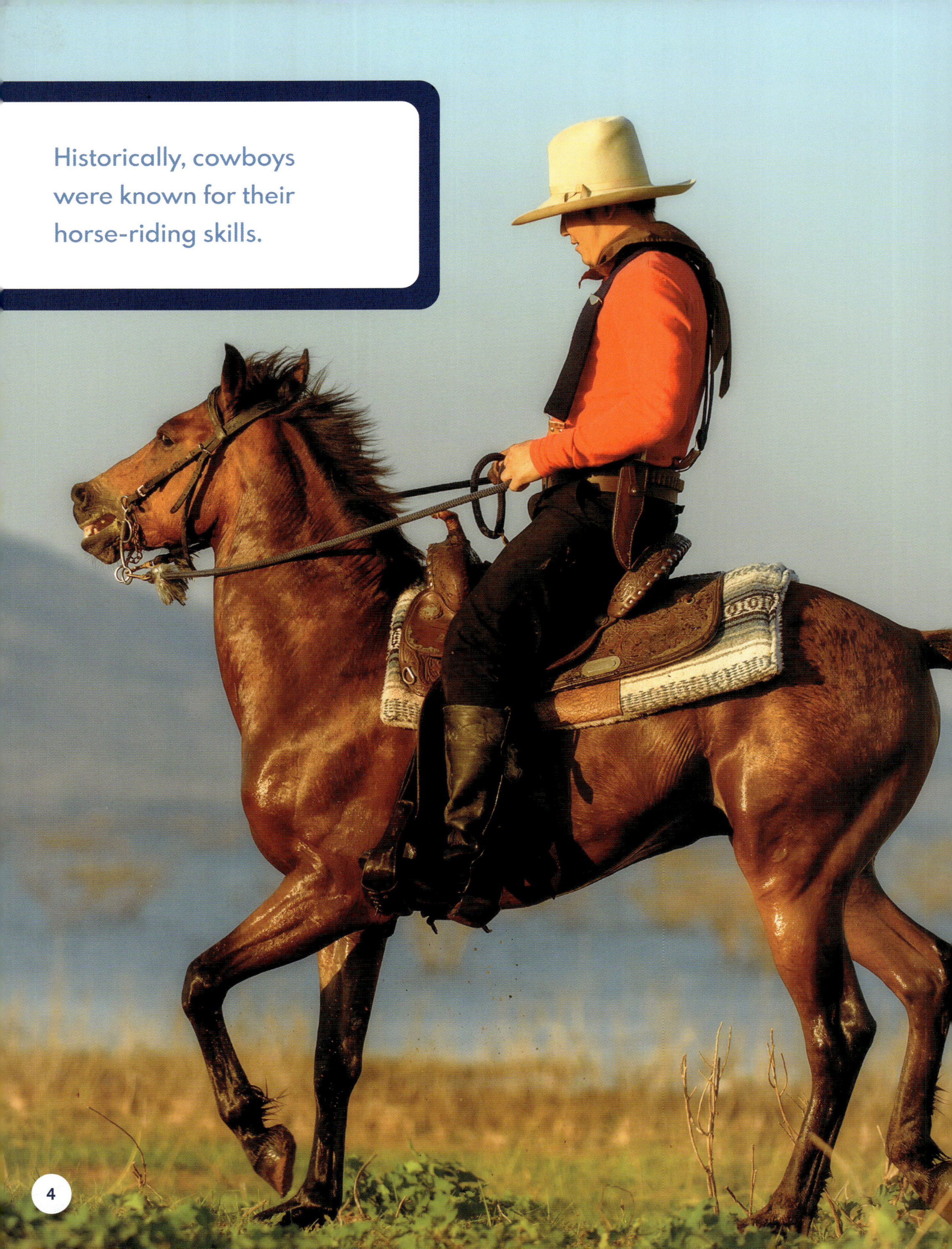
Historically, cowboys
were known for their
horse-riding skills.

CHAPTER 1

A Legendary Cowboy

Pecos Bill was the best cowboy in the West. He wore a cowboy hat and a bandana tied around his neck. He spent his time roping cattle and fighting bad men.

Usually, Pecos Bill rode on his horse. But it had been hurt.

Pecos Bill was alone. He walked on foot through the Texas desert.

Pecos Bill heard a rattling noise. He turned and saw a huge rattlesnake. It was ten feet (3 m) long and ready to fight. Pecos Bill wasn't scared. He knew he could handle it.

The snake struck. Pecos Bill was sure he would win. But he wanted the fight to be fair.

The Role of a Cowboy

Around 1865, the US beef industry began to grow. Many people in the Southwest started raising cattle. Cowboys were in charge of the cattle. They kept track of the cows, herded them, and cared for them. Eventually, cowboys sold their cattle on the market.

So Pecos Bill let the snake bite him three times
before he reacted. Then he grabbed the snake.
He whipped it around like a **lasso**. Pecos Bill
had bested the biggest rattlesnake in Texas.

Later, Pecos Bill ran into a mountain lion.
Again, he was unafraid. He tamed the mountain
lion in a few minutes. Pecos Bill rode into the
desert on the mountain lion's back.

Cowboys herd cattle, moving them to fields where there is more grass.

Western Tall Tales

Pecos Bill wasn't a real man. He is a character in many tall tales. These stories describe a cowboy who is larger than life. He is said to have lassoed an entire herd of cattle at once. In another tale, he rides a tornado as if it were a bucking bull.

Stories about Pecos Bill traveled through the US Southwest starting in the 1920s. At this time, the cowboy was a heroic figure in American culture. Cowboys represented values such as hard work, bravery, and strength. Pecos Bill was the ultimate cowboy.

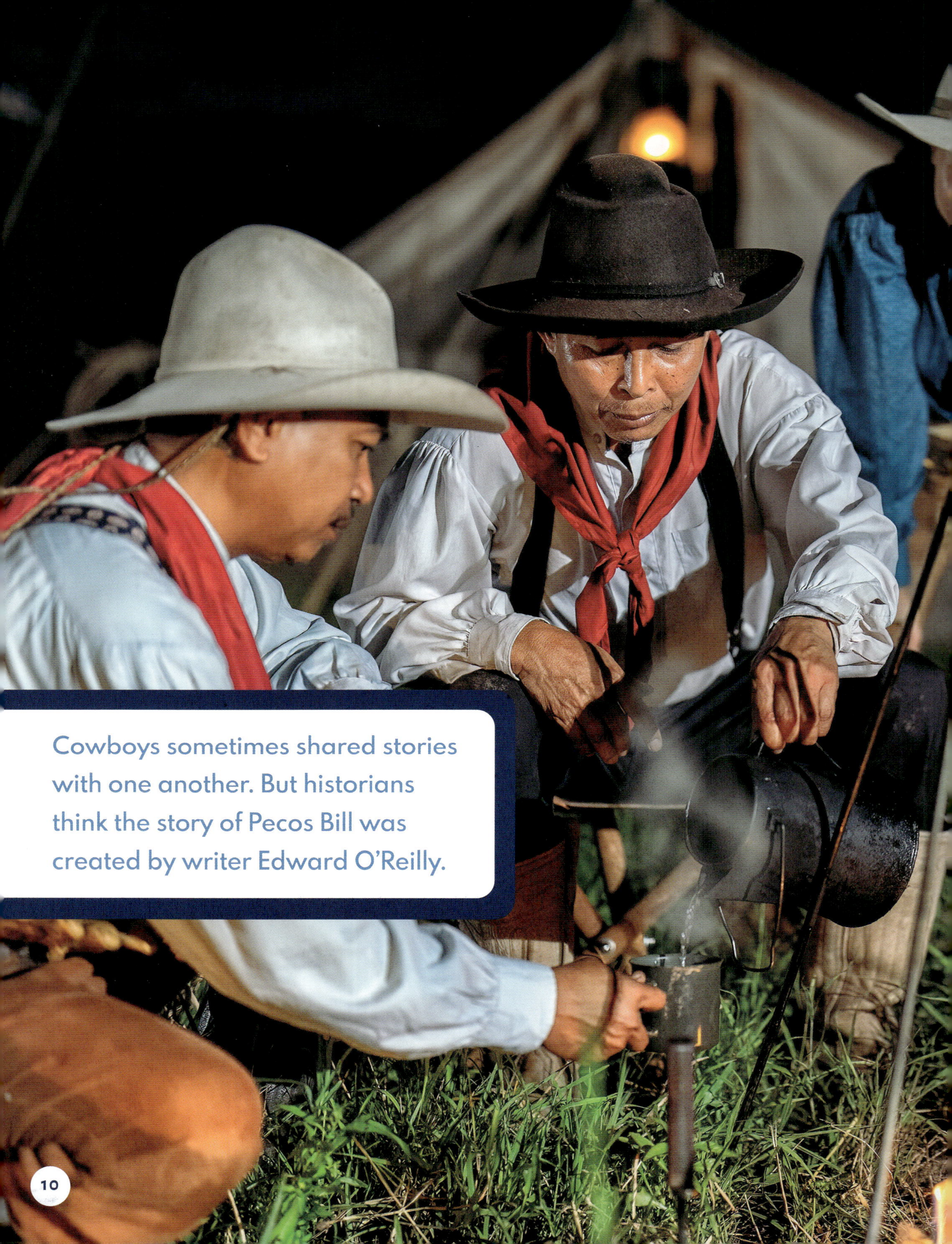

Cowboys sometimes shared stories with one another. But historians think the story of Pecos Bill was created by writer Edward O'Reilly.

CHAPTER 2

Bringing Pecos Bill to Life

The first story about Pecos Bill was published in 1923. Edward O'Reilly wrote "The Saga of Pecos Bill." He said that he heard stories about Pecos Bill from cowboys. But some people who study **folklore** say that O'Reilly made these stories up.

After O'Reilly's story came out, many other Pecos Bill stories followed. Most of them used similar details as the original tale. People also created comic strips about the cowboy.

The Life of Pecos Bill

In the stories, Pecos Bill was born in the 1830s. He was the youngest of 18 children. His parents were **pioneers**. One day, Pecos Bill's family was traveling across Texas in a covered wagon. Pecos Bill fell out. He was swept away by the Pecos River.

A pack of coyotes found Pecos Bill. They raised him as if he were a pup. Before he turned ten, he had learned how to howl and hunt. Pecos Bill believed he was a coyote. Then a

cowboy found him. The cowboy showed

Pecos Bill that he didn't have a tail like the

other coyotes. Pecos Bill went back to live

with humans.

Coyotes often live together in family groups and sometimes work together to hunt.

It wasn't long before Pecos Bill behaved like a cowboy himself. He got a horse and named it Widow Maker. The horse loved to eat dynamite.

Pecos Bill was the only person alive who was strong enough to ride Widow Maker.

One day, Pecos Bill saw a woman named Slue-Foot Sue. She was riding down a river called the Rio Grande. She rode a catfish as big as a whale. Pecos Bill fell in love, and he and Sue got married. Sue wanted to ride Widow Maker. Pecos Bill let her, but Sue wasn't strong enough.

No More Widow Maker

In one comic about Pecos Bill, Widow Maker doesn't exist. Instead, Pecos Bill's horse was named Dewdrop. In the story, Pecos Bill and Dewdrop entered a race. But Dewdrop was too tired to run. So Pecos Bill carried his horse through the whole race. They still won!

Widow Maker bucked Sue off. She flew all the way to the moon.

Some stories say Pecos Bill met a man from the North who wanted to look like a cowboy. He put on all sorts of fancy clothes. Pecos Bill thought the man looked so funny that he laughed himself to death.

Some tales about Pecos Bill reflect harmful **stereotypes** of the time. They show the negative ideas that some people had about American Indians and Mexicans. In one comic, Pecos Bill is kidnapped by a group of American Indians. They threaten to kill him, but Pecos Bill outsmarts them and escapes. The story depicts American Indians as unintelligent and violent.

Pecos Bill Lore and Landmarks

There was a drought in Texas. Pecos Bill lassoed a storm cloud from California. It rained so much that the **Gulf of Mexico** formed.

Pecos Bill once rode a tornado. It tried hard to shake him off. It was so strong that it carved the **Grand Canyon**.

Pecos Bill was eventually shaken from the tornado. When he hit the ground, the impact created **Death Valley**.

Pecos Bill got lost in the desert, and he didn't have anything to drink. So he dug the **Rio Grande**.

Pecos Bill is said to have helped create many famous landmarks in the Southwest. He formed them using his larger-than-life abilities.

Pecos Bill represents ideals such as toughness. But some of his stories also include harmful stereotypes.

Similar depictions of Mexicans appear in other stories. These stereotypes are untrue. Still, these famous stories turned Pecos Bill into a major figure in American folklore.

Primary Source

Many historians, including Brent Ashabranner, no longer believe that cowboys told stories about Pecos Bill. Ashabranner wrote:

> I have during the past five years examined scores of **memoirs** written . . . by old-time cowboys . . . and I have found in them no mention of . . . a character called Pecos Bill.

Source: Brent Ashabranner. "Pecos Bill: An Appraisal." *Western Folklore*, Jan. 1952, Vol. 11, No. 1, p. 21.

What's the Big Idea?

Read this quote carefully. What is its main idea? Explain how the main idea is supported by details.

Pecos Bill is shown riding his trusted horse in Disney's *Melody Time.*

Pecos Bill in Film

Stories about Pecos Bill have been told for decades. One of the first movies to show Pecos Bill was Disney's animated film *Melody Time*. It was released in 1948. It also showed other tall tales. Disney's version of Pecos Bill had similarities to O'Reilly's story.

Pecos Bill is tough and brave in *Melody Time.* He eats with coyotes, chases antelopes, and rests on top of a cactus's spikes. He fights off a group of 50 vultures trying to eat a horse. That is how he meets Widow Maker.

The film shows many of their adventures. Pecos Bill rides a cyclone, digs the Rio Grande, and ropes a group of men stealing cattle. He marries Slue-Foot Sue, and she is bounced to the moon. However, negative stereotypes about American Indians show up in *Melody Time* too.

Disney's *Tall Tale*

Disney released another movie about Pecos Bill in 1995. This one was called *Tall Tale.* It was a live-action movie with real actors.

In *Melody Time*, Pecos Bill lassos a storm and takes it to Texas. This ends a drought in the state.

The plot of *Tall Tale* is much different from earlier stories about Pecos Bill. The cowboy helps a young boy save his father's farm.

In Disney's live-action film *Tall Tale*, Pecos Bill, *right*, helps protect a farm.

They meet other characters from American folklore, such as Paul Bunyan and John Henry. These characters work together as a team.

In O'Reilly's stories, Pecos Bill is tough and independent. These were important values in the early United States. In *Tall Tale*, Pecos Bill is more **vulnerable**. He can't do everything on his own. Instead, he needs help from others. Pecos Bill and the boy save the farm through teamwork. They must believe in each other to succeed.

A Magic Tornado

In some stories, Pecos Bill rides a tornado to show off his strength. But in *Tall Tale*, Pecos Bill uses a tornado as a way to get around. In the film, he appears in the desert. He steps out of a small tornado. Later, he gifts Widow Maker to the young boy. He then disappears in another tornado.

In 1996, Pecos Bill was featured in a stamp collection with other heroes of US folklore.

American values changed over time. Being kind and working together became more important. Stories like Pecos Bill's have changed to reflect those values. Pecos Bill was not a real man. But stories about his life tell an important tale about the culture and history of the Southwest.

Further Evidence

Look at the website below. Does it give any new evidence about Pecos Bill's life to support Chapter Three?

Children's Story: "Pecos Bill"

abdocorelibrary.com/pecos-bill

Legendary Facts

Pecos Bill is a larger-than-life cowboy from American tall tales.

In some stories, Pecos Bill rode a horse named Widow Maker who ate dynamite.

Edward O'Reilly published the first story about Pecos Bill in 1923. It said Pecos Bill was raised by coyotes. He also fought a giant rattlesnake.

Disney released two movies about Pecos Bill. They were called *Melody Time* (1948) and *Tall Tale* (1995).

Glossary

folklore
traditional beliefs and stories from a community

lasso
a rope with a loop at the end that is used to catch cattle or horses

memoirs
nonfiction stories written from the author's personal memories or experiences

pioneers
people who are among the first to explore an area

stereotypes
beliefs that are oversimplified and usually not true

vulnerable
being emotionally open and accepting support or protection

Online Resources

To learn more about Pecos Bill and the US Southwest, visit our free resource websites below.

Visit **abdocorelibrary.com** or scan this QR code for free Common Core resources for teachers and students, including vetted activities, multimedia, and booklinks, for deeper subject comprehension.

Visit **abdobooklinks.com** or scan this QR code for free additional online weblinks for further learning. These links are routinely monitored and updated to provide the most current information available.

Learn More

Hudak, Heather C. *Paul Bunyan and Babe the Blue Ox.* Abdo, 2024.

Lowe, Mifflin. *The True West.* Bushel and Peck, 2020.

Richmond, Marley. *Calamity Jane.* Abdo, 2024.

Index

About the Author

Marley Richmond is a children's book editor and author. She lives in Minnesota with her cat, Bean.